My friend John Crotts is
tor. His biblical skill and p
thirty-one-day devotional ⎯, who
may be broken, hopeless, and despairing. Whether for use in
one's personal devotions, in a small group, or even as a counseling tool, this book has so much to commend it. John has excelled
in this devotional format, turning the angles of biblical hope like
a diamond, bringing forth the true hope we have in Jesus and his
hope-giving Word.

> —**Brian Borgman**, Founding Pastor, Grace Community
> Church, Minden, Nevada; Author, *Feelings and Faith* and
> *An Exile's Guide to Walking with God*

John Crotts is a faithful pastor and a skilled expositor. Both are well
reflected in this biblical and accessible thirty-one-day devotional
book, *Hope: Living Confidently in God*. John carefully chooses key
passages on this topic and pastorally applies them to highlight
the hope of the gospel and the confidence that knowing Christ
brings to our lives. The best part is how John's personal faith runs
as a thread throughout the whole book, bringing real and authentic wisdom and encouragement to the life of any Christian who
seeks to be reminded afresh of the unshakeable hope Christ provides in a broken world. I commend this book and its author.

> —**Brian Croft**, Founder and Executive Director, Practical
> Shepherding; Senior Fellow, Mathena Center for Church
> Revitalization, The Southern Baptist Theological Seminary

Hurting believers often lack hope, and their problems are typically
compounded by the fact that they are not consistently spending
time in God's Word. John Crotts's thirty-one-day devotional does
a wonderful job of addressing both needs. Through his decades of
pastoral experience, he understands the despair into which God's
people often fall. He faithfully applies God's Word to the hurting

soul, often drawing from passages profound insights that would not occur to most of us as remedies for hopelessness. This devotional will get the brother or sister who needs hope back into the Word on a daily basis through bite-sized portions.

—**Jim Newheiser**, Director of the Christian Counseling Program, Reformed Theological Seminary, Charlotte; Executive Director, The Institute for Biblical Counseling & Discipleship

John Crotts is my pastor, and he has written several books, and I have read them all. Two of his books have been my favorites, but now I have to add a third: *Hope.* Two words come to mind about this book: *sweet* and *comforting.* I highly recommend this book, as you will draw closer to God, and you will love it.

—**Martha Peace**, Certified Biblical Counselor; Author, *The Excellent Wife*

It has been said that without hope a person will fail to persevere. John has written what I'd like to call "spiritual B_{12} shots of hope." We all need hope—some more than others, depending on what is going on in life. I encourage readers of this great book to take their own "daily dose" of hope in God and his promises and to spread it around.

—**Stuart W. Scott**, Professor of Biblical Counseling, Graduate Program of The Master's University

"Hope begins with thinking right thoughts about God." This line from *Hope* summarizes the foundational truths about hope from God's Word found in these pages. Hope is essential to a well-lived life, and it is essential to biblical counseling. You cannot care for someone's soul without offering them hope. *Hope* is a wonderful companion, a co-counselor, to take with you into any counseling situation.

—**Curtis Solomon**, Executive Director, Biblical Counseling Coalition

HOPE

31-Day Devotionals for Life

A Series

Deepak Reju
Series Editor

Addictive Habits: Changing for Good, by David R. Dunham
After an Affair: Pursuing Restoration, by Michael Scott Gembola
Anger: Calming Your Heart, by Robert D. Jones
Anxiety: Knowing God's Peace, by Paul Tautges
Assurance: Resting in God's Salvation, by William P. Smith
Chronic Illness: Walking by Faith, by Esther Smith
Contentment: Seeing God's Goodness, by Megan Hill
Doubt: Trusting God's Promises, by Elyse Fitzpatrick
Engagement: Preparing for Marriage, by Mike McKinley
Fearing Others: Putting God First, by Zach Schlegel
Forgiveness: Reflecting God's Mercy, by Hayley Satrom
Grief: Walking with Jesus, by Bob Kellemen
Hope: Living Confidently in God, by John Crotts
Marriage Conflict: Talking as Teammates, by Steve Hoppe
Money: Seeking God's Wisdom, by Jim Newheiser
A Painful Past: Healing and Moving Forward, by Lauren Whitman
Parenting & Disabilities: Abiding in God's Presence,
by Stephanie O. Hubach
Patience: Waiting with Hope, by Megan Hill
Pornography: Fighting for Purity, by Deepak Reju
Singleness: Living Faithfully, by Jenilyn Swett
Toxic Relationships: Taking Refuge in Christ, by Ellen Mary Dykas

HOPE

LIVING
CONFIDENTLY
IN GOD

JOHN CROTTS

P&R
PUBLISHING
P.O. BOX 817 • PHILLIPSBURG • NEW JERSEY 08865-0817

Printed in the United States of America

Library of Congress Cataloging-in-Publication Data

Names: Crotts, John, 1968- author.
Title: Hope : living confidently in God / John Crotts.
Description: Phillipsburg, New Jersey : P&R Publishing, 2021. | Series:
   31-day devotionals for life | Summary: "Christian hope isn't
   self-made-it's a sustaining certainty because it's based on God's
   promises, not wishful thinking. Strengthen your heart with hope through
   31 devotional readings and practical exercises"-- Provided by publisher.
   Identifiers: LCCN 2020012355 | ISBN 9781629957371 (paperback) | ISBN
   9781629957388 (epub) | ISBN 9781629957395 (mobi)
Subjects: LCSH: Hope--Biblical teaching. | Hope--Religious
   aspects--Christianity.
Classification: LCC BS680.H7 C76 2020 | DDC 242--dc23
LC record available at https://lccn.loc.gov/2020012355

To Joshua and Charissa Koh.
May the Lord give you a family filled with hope!

Contents

How to Nourish Your Soul   9

Introduction   11

The Beginning of Hope

Day 1: Where Hope Begins   17

Day 2: The Spiritual Connection between Faith and Hope   19

Jesus Is Your Hope

Day 3: Jesus, the Anchor of the Soul   23

Day 4: The Certainty of Jesus   25

Day 5: Jesus Cares about Your Troubles   27

Day 6: Jesus Has the Power and the Heart to Help   29

Day 7: Jesus Loves Desperate Sinners   31

Day 8: Jesus Is Merciful to the Very End   33

Day 9: Jesus Restores after Massive Sin   35

God's Character Sustains Hope

Day 10: Your God Is the Living God   39

Day 11: God Is for You   41

Day 12: God Delights in the Hopeful   43

Day 13: God Is Sovereign   45

Day 14: God's Resurrection Power Brings Hope   47

Day 15: God Is More Gracious Than You Can Imagine   49

Day 16: God Himself Will Get Us Through   51

Day 17: Our Omnipotent God Cares   53

Day 18: The Lord Is Worth the Wait   55

You Can Face Life's Difficulties with Hope

Day 19: When You Feel Financial Pressure   59

Day 20: When a Relationship Is Broken   61

Day 21: When Your Options Run Out   63

Day 22: When Your World Collapses   65

Day 23: When Your Hopes Are Dashed   67

Day 24: When You Are Struggling with Sin   69

Day 25: When You Feel Abandoned by God   71

Day 26: When You Wrestle with Despair   73

Day 27: When a Believing Loved One Dies   75

Hope in the End

Day 28: Because He Lives   79

Day 29: The Blessed Hope of Christ's Return   81

Day 30: Heaven on Earth   83

Day 31: Ultimate Hope   85

Conclusion   87

Acknowledgments   89

Suggested Resources for the Journey   91

How to Nourish Your Soul

A LITTLE BIT every day can do great good for your soul.

I read the Bible to my kids during breakfast. I don't read a lot. Maybe just a few verses. But I work hard to do it every weekday.

My wife and I pray for one of our children, every night, before we go to bed. We usually take just a few minutes. We don't pray lengthy, expansive prayers. But we try to do this most every night.

Although they don't take long, these practices are edifying, hopeful, and effective.

This devotional is just the same. Each entry is short. Just a few tasty morsels of Scripture to nourish your starving soul. Read it on the subway or the bus on the way to work. Read it with a friend or a spouse every night at dinner. Make it a part of each day for thirty-one days, and it will do you great good.

Why is that?

We start with Scripture. God's Word is powerful. Used by the Holy Spirit, it turns the hearts of kings, brings comfort to the lowly, and gives spiritual sight to the blind. It transforms lives and turns them upside down. We know that the Bible is God's very own words, so we read and study it to know God himself.

Our study of Scripture is practical. Theology should change how we live. It's crucial to connect the Word with your daily life. Often, as you read this devotional, you'll see the word *you* because John speaks directly to you, the reader. Each devotional contains at least one reflection question and practical suggestion. You'll get much more from this experience if you answer the questions and do the practical exercises. Don't skip them. Do them for the sake of your own soul.

Our study of Scripture is worshipful. The Bible is overflowing with hope because real hope is found in God and in his gospel news about his beloved Son, Jesus. Christ died for your sins and will return again one day to bring you back with him to the Father. This hope is gritty and long-lasting. It gets you out of bed in the morning, gives you genuine joy and contentment, and helps you to weather the worst storms. It inspires worship every day of the week, not just on Sundays. And it won't let you down.

Are you ready for something like this? You probably need it just as much as I do.

If you find this devotional helpful (and I trust that you will!), reread it in different seasons of your life. It will help to remind you of God's goodness and power and promises, both in good seasons and in bad. So work through it this coming month and then come back to it a year from now to remind yourself about what God and the gospel teach us about hope.

This devotional starts you on a wonderful journey toward hope. If, after reading and rereading it, you want more gospel-rich resources about hope, John has listed several at the end of the book. Buy them and make good use of them.

Are you ready? Let's begin.

Deepak Reju

Introduction

IF YOU HOLD a penny right up to your eye, it appears huge—it is all you can see. In the same way, the problems in front of you are often painfully magnified, dominating your vision. An unexpected loss of income, a relationship that feels ruined, a doctor saying "cancer," the feeling that you are at the bottom of a well of sinful choices and their devastating consequences—all can overload your perspective. How can you think of anything else?

When you take that penny away from your eyes, though, perspective returns. It is still every bit a penny, but lying on the table, the penny doesn't seem so enormous. Having a hopeful perspective is a vital ingredient for enduring even the hardest problems of life with joy. As you lower the trial from right before your eyes, what do you now see? You see God. You see his love, his power, his plan, his faithfulness, his complete control. As right views of God fill your field of vision, something will seem different. You have hope.

What Is Hope?

Hope is confidence for a better future. If a person doesn't expect a better outcome in the future, they become stuck in present bleakness. The farmer works hard on his rugged land in hope of some kind of future harvest. If he didn't assume a harvest, there would be no need for him to fight the weeds.

Sadly, many people try to function with an optimistic attitude about the future without any real basis for their good expectations. Against a world filled with hard things, those desperate for hope clasp at any positive platitude. If your self-made reasons for hope are insufficient to survive the circumstance, your hope is really wishful thinking. No amount of wishing will enable you to swim across the sea.

Real, biblical hope is different. The resources for your expectations are not in yourself but in God. Because God is infinite in all of his attributes, those who trust in him have solid assurance of his goodness toward them for the future. Christian hope is confident. All the faith you rightly have in God as he is revealed in the Bible is aimed at your future. This future-oriented faith is true hope, and it will never fail.

The God of hope has unlimited power. As the angel Gabriel declared to Mary that she, a virgin, would become pregnant with the Son of God, he said, "Nothing will be impossible with God" (Luke 1:37). There is no problem that is too big for God to get a person through. God can change an entire nation in a day; he can always strengthen you.

The God of hope also has clear purposes and a big plan. He is working everything according to the counsel of his will (see Eph. 1:11). His sovereign plan and his providential control of the outworking of his plan extend to the very details of your life. That means that your suffering is never meaningless. God is at work. We can't always know all that God is doing, but we can be certain that he is working in your trial (see Rom. 8:28). If we knew all that he was accomplishing, we would bow before him in awe of his plan.

The God of hope has blessed us with wonderful promises to help us to hope. His promises reveal his character and his heart. God is true and unchanging; therefore, every word he has given us in the Bible is reliable. His promises give us confidence that he is with us and that he will always give us grace to endure the trial (see 1 Cor. 10:13). The God of hope truly cares for his people. He is not like a supercomputer calculating your problems and spitting out solutions. God loves you. God is working in and around your difficult life situations in personal ways.

Facing your problems with biblical hope does not guarantee

that you will see positive outcomes on all of your trials. But God will help you in your trials. He may not change your outward circumstances, but he will use his truth to lift your heart. Your hope-filled heart will help you to honor him and to endure through every trial. Whatever God doesn't fix in this short life will be more than made up for through all eternity.

The Purpose of This Book

This devotional is not a Bible study about hope. Instead, each day brings you a different encouragement from Scripture designed to inspire you to hope. There are all kinds of problems that you will face in this life—all of them need hope. The Bible contains all kinds of ways that God inspires us to hope in him—direct statements, psalms sung in troubled times, promises, and even familiar stories. Don't rush past any of the meditations. Take time to reflect upon the Scriptures and to put into practice the practical suggestions as you are able. Consider how each meditation could inspire more hope in you. Ask the Lord to fill your heart with hope. God will help you.

Each day you will see a different facet of the diamond of God's character. It is my prayer that the fresh rays of hope that you receive from God's Word in the next thirty-one days will become a bright, shining beam of hope radiating from your heart.

THE BEGINNING
OF HOPE

DAY 1

Where Hope Begins

According to [God's] great mercy, he has caused us to be born again to a living hope through the resurrection of Jesus Christ from the dead, to an inheritance that is imperishable, undefiled, and unfading, kept in heaven for you, who by God's power are being guarded through faith for a salvation ready to be revealed in the last time. (1 Peter 1:3–5)

WHAT WORDS DO you associate with your salvation?

Christians usually associate salvation from God's judgment with the word *faith*. After all, the Bible says you can never earn salvation through good works: salvation is received by faith alone. The Lord Jesus has done the work. He lived righteously. He died in the place of sinners on the cross. He rose from the dead. Jesus calls people to stop trusting their own righteousness and to put their faith in him alone. That is what it means to be a Christian.

But *hope* is also a wonderful salvation word.

People usually use the word *hope* to mean an optimistic or positive wish for the future. Sometimes the biblical writers use *hope* in this way, like when Paul says to Timothy, "I hope to come to you soon" (1 Tim. 3:14). In that situation, Paul didn't know what God had planned and wished for a speedy visit to his friend.

For a non-Christian, wishful hope is the best they can have. A Christian has a far more powerful hope, however: the hope that comes through salvation. Because Jesus rose from the dead, your trust in him is not in vain. He proved the reality of the world to come. When he brings you to heaven, your hopes will be filled with substance. You may never receive an earthly inheritance, but you will receive a heavenly inheritance in glory. It will never perish, become defiled, or fade away. You will never get such assurances from earthly treasures. You can be confident about your heavenly inheritance because God is personally guarding it until you receive it.

Although you deserve God's punishment because of your sinful attitudes and actions, God has given you mercy—*great mercy*, in fact. In that great mercy he has caused you to be *born again*, to come to life spiritually. As your spiritual eyes open, you begin to see through lenses of hope—dynamic *living hope*. When God changes you from a rebellious creature into an adopted son, you can have confidence, even certainty, that God will accomplish good plans in your life. You can have confident expectations of the future, the very meaning of hope.

Because of your salvation, you have a solid foundation for hope.

Reflect: In the Roman world, the apostle Paul frequently saw soldiers in armor. Once he illustrated spiritual warfare by calling Christians to use "for a helmet the hope of salvation" (1 Thess. 5:8). In both physical and spiritual battle, protection for the head is essential. What are some ways your salvation hope straps on like a secure helmet for protection in the battles you face?

Act: Write 1 Peter 1:3–5 on an index card and place it on your bathroom mirror. Read it over every morning for these thirty-one days to impress its truth on your heart.

DAY 2

The Spiritual Connection
between Faith and Hope

*Now faith is the assurance of things hoped for, the
conviction of things not seen. (Heb. 11:1)*

THE WORD HOPE is popularly used for something good a person wishes for in the future. *Faith* is belief or trust in a person, idea, or thing. The Bible, however, fills both of these words with greater significance.

As we saw yesterday, the gospel says that sinners are declared righteous by faith alone in Christ alone. Your faith is only as good as its object—our Savior, Jesus. Your sins had separated you from your perfect Creator. You were a condemned criminal before a judge. You couldn't do enough good deeds to earn God's favor. But Jesus offered to take the punishment you deserve. When you trust in Christ, you receive him and his gift of mercy: "the free gift of God is eternal life in Christ Jesus our Lord" (Rom. 6:23).

Faith in Christ is more than just mentally believing a series of facts about him. Faith is *confidence* in the Lord Jesus Christ—who he is and what he has done—and all that the Bible says about him. Although you haven't seen him, you have conviction that he is the Lord who rose from the dead.

Hope is future-oriented faith. Hope, like faith, is confidence in the Lord Jesus and all that the Bible says about him, but it is confidence aimed at the future. Jesus will come again as he promised. He will rescue his people and judge the world. He will bring this world back to life. He will bring heaven to earth, and Christians will be with the Lord forever. His promises are reliable. The final salvation of believers is sure and glorious.

Biblical *hope* is more than wishful thinking. Biblical hope is an assured expectation that everything God has promised will come to pass. God cannot lie. All that the Bible says is true, and the future its words describe is as certain as if it had already happened.

People all around us use the words *faith* and *hope*, but only those who believe the Bible understand the true weight of these precious words.

Reflect: Does your understanding of hope match the popular meaning of wishing for future good or the biblical understanding of confident expectations of the future based upon God's character and promises?

Reflect: The apostle Paul frequently thanks God for virtues manifested in Christians he knows. One of those virtues is hope. "We give thanks to God always for all of you, constantly mentioning you in our prayers, remembering before our God and Father your work of faith and labor of love and steadfastness of hope in our Lord Jesus Christ" (1 Thess. 1:2–3). Who models this kind of Christian hope in your life? How has that person's hope encouraged you? Can you give thanks to God for them?

Act: If you don't have the kind of faith and hope the Bible talks about, ask God to give them to you.

JESUS IS YOUR HOPE

DAY 3

Jesus, the Anchor of the Soul

*When God desired to show . . . the unchangeable character
of his purpose, he guaranteed it with an oath, so that by two
unchangeable things, in which it is impossible for God to lie, we
. . . might have strong encouragement to hold fast to the hope set
before us. We have this as a sure and steadfast anchor of the soul,
a hope that enters into the inner place behind the curtain, where
Jesus has gone as a forerunner on our behalf. (Heb. 6:17–20)*

HAVE YOU EVER felt like you were drifting along through life?
I don't mean feeling as though you're just reacting to life's events
without a plan. I mean feeling spiritually purposeless or even
drifting away from God. Perhaps you are there right now.

Maybe you grew up around the things of God—Bible stories,
joyful songs, and good people who walked with God. Those days
seem like a lifetime ago. God seems far away, and darkness seems
to be closing in. One more storm might push your ship so far off
course that you can't get back.

Is there an anchor to stabilize your life and to keep you close
to God? Could the things of God that you remember return as
reality to keep life's storms from destroying you? Is a better future
beyond the ominous clouds on the horizon?

It is not too late. The Bible assures you that the Lord Jesus is
strong enough to change you from the inside out. He can not only
fully forgive your bad choices but also adopt you into his family,
fill you with internal joy no matter what you are enduring, and
one day welcome you into eternal life in the new heavens and the
new earth.

The author of Hebrews wanted to encourage a group of Jews
who had trusted in Christ to endure a coming onslaught of Roman

persecution. The persecution promised to be so severe that some of their lives would be threatened. The Hebrews were spiritually wavering, and some were drifting from the things of God.

To infuse massive hope into these troubled souls, he reminded them of the character of God. *God cannot lie.* Plus, this God has made *unchangeable oaths* about the truthfulness of his *promises.* These strong assurances can put ballast in your ship and keep it upright. As bad as the coming storms may be, do not lose heart, because God will never let your ship topple in the sea of darkness. The Lord Jesus accomplished the work of salvation and returned in triumph to heaven. His person and work are the promises that you cling to: the sure and steadfast anchor of your soul.

For a drifting ship, the anchor plunges down from the deck into black waters below. The Lord Jesus Christ, though, is an anchor extending up into heaven itself. Heaven is a place of perfection, but though your life has been anything but perfect, you can go there. When you trust Christ, he wraps you in a robe of his righteousness. Now as you wait for the day when your faith becomes sight, *you have hope.* You have hope as strong as an anchor that keeps your soul from drifting in life's storms. You have hope that redirects your present life into endurance, comfort, and spiritual purpose.

Reflect: What are some ways you feel storm tossed? Which of the reasons are your sins and which are your circumstances?

Act: Look up a picture of a navy ship's anchor. Consider the strength of that anchor and its ability to hold fast such a massive ship. List ways the Lord Jesus Christ is an anchor for your soul. List ways God's promises act as ballast for life's storms.

DAY 4

The Certainty of Jesus

Jesus Christ is the same yesterday and today and forever. (Heb. 13:8)

THE INCONSISTENCIES OF life affect your hope. Your family may be getting along well, but then someone becomes sick, another has terrible trouble in school, and finally comes the firing. Even if your situation remains the same, your responses fluctuate. Hope seems impossible to maintain.

In spite of the uncertainties in this world, the Lord Jesus Christ is perfectly constant. He always has been, he is right now, and he always will be the same.

The Hebrews were professing Christians who faced persecution so severe that they were tempted to forsake the Lord and to return to Judaism. The author of the letter to the Hebrews used the constancy of Christ to inspire their hope.

After urging his readers to remember the faithful leaders whom they had seen persevere and to imitate their faith (see Heb. 13:7), he elevates the example to Jesus. Leaders live and die. Leaders can be faithful but will all falter from time to time. The Lord Jesus never changes.

When we have a lot of hope in an unstable object, our hope will eventually be dashed. No matter how confident I am that a child's plastic vehicle will hold my weight as a fully grown man, I will be disappointed at the eventual outcome. The Lord Jesus, however, is a solid rock to hope upon. Because his person and work never change (and never will), not only can your hope be sustained today, but you can know that it will hold forever.

The word *yesterday* looks back to the Lord's life and ministry on the earth, and even to eternity past. He has been faithful, and his words and works continue to be reliable.

Today, the Lord is at God's right hand. He is the sympathetic High Priest who welcomes his hopeful children to come to God because of his work on their behalf (see Heb. 4:14–16).

Because Jesus will be the same forever, we can know that his prayers for us will never stop until we are brought all the way to glory (see Heb. 7:25).

Although your life will shift and you will change, the Lord Jesus Christ will always remain the same. Because he is constant, your hope can continue. Because your hope continues, you can continue to follow the Lord.

Reflect: Everything great about Jesus (which is everything!) is permanent. His power and his love toward you will never be upgraded, because they are already complete. Here is sustained hope.

Act: Look up the lyrics to the hymn "My Hope is Built on Nothing Less." Worship the Lord by singing these words, which magnify the changeless certainty of the solid Rock of Christ.

DAY 5

Jesus Cares about Your Troubles

Therefore he had to be made like his brothers in every respect,
so that he might become a merciful and faithful high priest in
the service of God, to make propitiation for the sins of the people.
For because he himself has suffered when tempted, he is able
to help those who are being tempted. (Heb. 2:17–18)

A SUDDEN FINANCIAL CRISIS, a long-term health problem, or a lingering family conflict can wear a person out. Facing such trials with no one who can relate makes them feel unbearable. Trials blur into temptations. It can be so hard to keep responding to pain without sinfully reacting. In tough times, your sinful heart often deceives you into thinking no one else understands your pain. But is that true? Are you enduring your trial all by yourself?

Most have someone who cares for them, whether a family member, friend, or coworker. Christians ought to have an entire church family ready to help them to carry the load. But beyond earthly help, the Lord Jesus himself directly relates to us in our trials.

He is the Son of God, but he took on humanity, in part so that he could live among us. The trials he experienced on earth were so intense that he can always relate to you in your suffering. Even if Jesus didn't experience the exact same trial or give in to sinful reactions, what he did endure counts. He endured these fires so that he can come to your aid.

In a pressure cooker, steam builds and builds until it is finally released. Trials and temptations are like that, but even amidst trials, Jesus never sinned—he never used the release valve on the pressure cooker of his temptations.

As the devil himself attacked Jesus in the wilderness over

27

forty lonely, hungry days, Jesus continued to honor God. The devil intensified the pressure, and Jesus intensified his faithful endurance. Because Jesus never sinned, the satanic pressure of temptation far surpassed normal human levels. Part of why God subjected Jesus to such temptations was so that Jesus can honestly tell you that he relates to you in your times of temptation.

The Lord Jesus genuinely cares about you in your specific situation. Don't ever relegate God to the clouds and conclude that he relates to you only out of his deity. Jesus walked down the same dirty paths you walk. As the author of Hebrews says, Jesus was "made like his brothers in every respect." He was surrounded by painful circumstances and the same kinds of unconcerned people who surround you. Jesus was betrayed by his friend. He gets it. He truly does.

When you pray through severe pain with tear-stained eyes, you are talking to One who truly understands and cares. Jesus can help you. He wants to help you. He knows how to help you. He will help you. Here is real hope.

Reflect: Have you been tempted to believe that even Jesus doesn't understand your struggles?

Act: Make this prayer of hope your own: "It truly is a comfort to realize that Jesus understands my situation. I confess that I have felt completely alone in my trial. My aloneness has been a big part of my desperation. But I am not alone. I have never been alone. Jesus's trials and temptations on the earth were so powerful that he can relate to me. Thank you, Jesus, for wanting to relate to me. Thank you for your practical help. I need your help. You get it. You have told me that you are willing and able to help. Please help right now. I believe that you will, but help me to keep believing it! Amen."

DAY 6

Jesus Has the Power
and the Heart to Help

*For she said, "If I touch even his garments, I will be made well."
And immediately the flow of blood dried up, and she felt in her
body that she was healed of her disease. (Mark 5:28–29)*

THE FLU CAN make a person miserable for a week. Fights with cancer can go on for months and years. While people usually rise to the challenge of short-term trials, it is harder to hope when trials persist.

Today we read about a woman who knew this well. Scripture doesn't name her, but let's imagine she was named Sarah, after Abraham's famous wife. After twelve years of bleeding, Sarah could see no happy ending. She had done all that she could. She "had suffered much under many physicians, and had spent all that she had, and was no better but rather grew worse" (Mark 5:26).

Her double dilemma was debilitating hemorrhaging plus ostracism by the religious community (see Lev. 15:25–28). Without supportive friends, her pain increased. How long did God expect Sarah to keep hoping in him? Maybe like Sarah you too have been going through a trial that feels unending and impossible. You wonder how you can endure another day.

But Sarah heard about Jesus, and her dead hope awakened. Hope got Sarah out of her house and onto the streets. Hope fought feelings of shame and fear. She secretly approached Jesus while he was crushed in a mob of people.

The moment she touched the corner of Jesus's garment, Sarah was healed. Twelve years of pain and shame evaporated instantly. She thought, "If I touch even his garments, I will be made well." She was right. Her blood flow stopped. She felt it happen.

In spite of the crowd, Jesus didn't let that moment pass. With compassion and kindness, he affirmed her: "Daughter, your faith has made you well; go in peace, and be healed of your disease" (Mark 5:34).

Even when this woman surprised Jesus in his earthly ministry with her hopeful touch, God was not surprised. He knew all about the woman, her massive, long-term suffering, her many prayers, her doctor visits, her friendlessness, and her financial situation. He loved her. And through Jesus, he healed her on the spot.

Your drawn-out time of testing may have you down on your back physically, emotionally exhausted, or spiritually discouraged. As hope lifts you up to go to Jesus, know that he already knows the depth of your trial. He cares. He is at work in so many ways. Reach out to the One with the power to change things.

Reflect: The Lord Jesus Christ has the same power and authority he had in the Gospels. He can still be trusted. Even if he does not bring immediate healing, he will sustain your weak heart as he holds it close to his own. Think about him working out his wise plans in your trials. What good things has he done for you thus far in your trial? What else might he be accomplishing? He has the power to end your trial today, but he may be working toward a more glorious end. When you see him, you will agree that his plan was best and that he earned every ounce of your hope.

Act: Read Mark 5:24–34 and compare the bleeding woman's sufferings with your own. List ways that yours are similar to and distinct from hers. List ways the Lord Jesus cared for her and is caring for you.

DAY 7

Jesus Loves Desperate Sinners

*So he ran on ahead and climbed up into a sycamore tree to see him,
for he was about to pass that way. And when Jesus came to the
place, he looked up and said to him, "Zacchaeus, hurry and come
down, for I must stay at your house today." (Luke 19:4–5)*

MANY WOULD HAVE considered Zacchaeus successful and
wished to trade checkbooks with him. Zacchaeus was rich and
powerful, but he was also empty—achieving his status meant
paying a high price socially and spiritually. To maintain its power,
the Roman empire heavily taxed the people it conquered and sold
tax positions to natives who collected the taxes. These tax collec-
tors could overcharge their countrymen and pocket the surplus
with Rome's full support.

Working for the Romans was bad enough, but using the
Roman military to extort money from fellow Jews was unthink-
able. It was a betrayal. The Bible describes Zacchaeus as a "chief
tax collector." Apparently, the little guy was the big cheese. He
was stationed in Jericho, a city that fell along a major trade route,
and could thus collect large revenues. Abusing your position for
gain has implications for your social and spiritual life. If you did
both of those things in God's own nation of Israel, the social and
spiritual implications would be multiplied.

This filthy rich, filthy man apparently began to feel his filthi-
ness. I say that because he wanted to see Jesus. He *really* wanted
to see Jesus.

In Eastern cultures like Israel's, honor and shame are so
important that people would rather be respected than be right.
Zacchaeus wanted to see Jesus enough to shamefully climb a tree.
Zacchaeus was too short to see Jesus through the crowds and too

31

despised for anyone to let him through. He wanted to see Jesus so badly that he ran ahead and found the sycamore tree. The Bible doesn't say what he heard about Jesus or what he was hoping to get from seeing Jesus. We do know he was hated in Israel, and we know he was desperate to see Jesus.

Is there hope for such a man? After all, his heart was hard enough to take the tax job. He advanced in his wicked occupation to become the chief of the lot. God's people bitterly hated betrayers like him. Perhaps it wouldn't be surprising if Jesus spit on such a sinner.

Of course, Jesus didn't spit on this desperate man. He stopped at the tree Zacchaeus had climbed, called Zacchaeus by name, and invited himself over for lunch. I'm sure Zacchaeus was shocked. He hurriedly climbed back down the tree and received Jesus joyfully.

So many tongues wagged simultaneously that I wonder if you could feel the warm wind along Jericho's main street. The crowd couldn't believe Jesus would stoop to eat with one who had stooped so morally low as to harm his own people. Jesus loves desperate sinners. Especially sinners who realize their desperation, like Zacchaeus.

Reflect: Before he met Jesus, Zacchaeus's lust for money surpassed his desires to be a part of God's people. But Zacchaeus's new generosity was visible proof that Jesus had changed him. He told Jesus, "Behold, Lord, the half of my goods I give to the poor. And if I have defrauded anyone of anything, I restore it fourfold" (Luke 19:8). This was not an effort to buy God's favor but rather evidence that this desperate man had had a life-changing encounter with Jesus.

Act: Read Luke 19:1–10. List how you are like Zacchaeus. List ways that Jesus's dealings with Zacchaeus inspire your hope.

DAY 8

Jesus Is Merciful to the Very End

And he said, "Jesus, remember me when you come into your kingdom." And he said to him, "Truly, I say to you, today you will be with me in paradise." (Luke 23:42–43)

IN THE FOUR GOSPELS, Jesus leaves a trail of mercy behind him. *Oh, you're a blind beggar? Oh, you're infested with demons? Oh, you sell your body for money? Oh, you're the town drunk? It's nice to meet you; I'm Jesus.* The next thing you know, even huge sins are forgiven and people are on their feet again. Right with God, they begin to get right with the world. They have new purpose and direction.

But these people had time to turn things around. Perhaps you don't think you have enough time left to turn the right way. Your parents told you about Jesus. Your church friends continued the lessons. But you wouldn't listen. And you wonder if it is too late. If you've spent your life rebelling against God, you are right to be concerned. But there is hope even for you.

The Bible records that Jesus died between two convicted robbers. The passersby mocked Jesus, and even the criminals joined in. How hard must their hearts have been to mock the man being crucified beside them?

Crucifixion chokes its victims. Every gulp of air becomes more labored and painful. Yet in his suffering, Jesus pushed out a prayer for mercy: "Father, forgive them, for they know not what they do" (Luke 23:34).

As the minutes wore on, his mercy melted one of the robbers. He pointed out to his partner in crime that they were experiencing justice, but Jesus had done nothing wrong. Then he asked Jesus, "Remember me when you come into your kingdom."

Jesus's reply is nothing less than astonishing: "Truly, I say to you, today you will be with me in paradise." Jesus made a solemn oath that this dying criminal would be with him that very day in the garden of God, heaven.

This man had stolen things from innocent victims. His crucifixion suggests that he had committed some supersized crimes. In Israel, you weren't put on a cross for taking figs from the fruit stand when you were starving. He was a hardened man who had spent his life rebelling against God. He had only a few hours left to repent before his eternal judgment was set in stone.

But he did repent. His words reveal real repentance and faith. He fully admitted his guilt (no more excuses, no more victim mentality). He even said he deserved to be crucified. Then he spoke to Jesus. His words show faith in who Jesus was (the King), where Jesus was going (heaven), and what Jesus could do (remember him). Christ had mercy on the thief's entire life and brought him along to paradise.

This man had nothing to offer Jesus, yet Jesus had mercy on him. Jesus even promised him that he would follow through. The Bible doesn't contain another story like this, but it does contain this story with its sliver of hope. If the clock is still moving, there is still time for you to have peace with God. You may not have much time left, but it is enough. Grab that sliver of hope. It is for you.

Reflect: How was Jesus's declaration "Today you will be with me" more merciful to the thief than forgiving him without such a declaration?

Reflect: How is this same declaration merciful to you?

Act: Respond to the hope this story offers. Add thanksgiving to your prayers for what Jesus did for the thief and how his mercy speaks to your life.

DAY 9

Jesus Restores after Massive Sin

When they had finished breakfast, Jesus said to Simon Peter, "Simon, son of John, do you love me more than these?" He said to him, "Yes, Lord; you know that I love you." He said to him, "Feed my lambs." (John 21:15)

DOES IT SEEM like Jesus leaves you alone in your fights sometimes? You can find hope in his dealings with Peter before, during, and after Peter's fight with Satan.

Jesus cared about Peter, even in the face of his own approaching trial. Before Peter fought the devil, Jesus prepared him. He described the temptation and assured Peter he was praying for his faith. He told Peter that although he would lose the fight, a better future was coming: "Behold, Satan demanded to have you, that he might sift you like wheat, but I have prayed for you that your faith may not fail. And when you have turned again, strengthen your brothers" (Luke 22:31–32).

When Jesus was arrested, Peter and John trailed the Roman soldiers into the courtyard outside the trial. The pressure in the room was high, but so was the pressure in the courtyard. Once, twice, three times, people suspiciously accused Peter of being connected to the man on trial. Once, twice, three times, Peter denied knowing Jesus.

As the rooster crowed, Jesus turned and caught Peter's eye. Peter's conscience was speared: the devil had bested him. Although Jesus's death was approaching, he was still concerned for Peter's soul.

Once he heard about Jesus's resurrection, Peter's heart must have held both marveling hope and crushing guilt. The Lord knew that Peter was mortified and had his angel single out Peter when announcing the news to Mary Magdalene: "But go, tell his disciples and Peter that he is going before you to Galilee" (Mark 16:7).

Later, a few disciples joined Peter on a fishing trip in Galilee. Jesus appeared to them on the shoreline, and a miraculous haul of fish revealed it was him. Peter scurried into the Sea of Galilee to get to Jesus as quickly as he could.

Three times, Jesus asked Peter, "Do you love me?" Three times, once for each denial, Peter affirmed his love for Jesus, and the Lord told him to feed his lambs, to tend his sheep, to feed his sheep, and to follow him.

Consider how much Jesus cared for Peter. He dealt so tenderly with Peter in a trial he knew Peter would fail. He prepared him. He encouraged him, in spite of his overconfidence. Jesus looked past his own pain to Peter at Peter's moment of failure. Jesus sent word to Peter by name after rising from the dead. He took him aside after the resurrection to assure him of his forgiveness and future usefulness.

Reflect: If you have fallen, have you repented? Jesus still knows you and cares for you. Tears of repentance may need to fall, but that's okay. The Lord loves to forgive his children. Your spiritual life is not over.

Act: Turn Peter's story of failure and restoration into specific prayers. Connect your story with Peter's intentions, confidence, failure, shame, and restoration.

GOD'S CHARACTER SUSTAINS HOPE

DAY 10

Your God Is the Living God

For whatever was written in former days was written for our instruction, that through endurance and through the encouragement of the Scriptures we might have hope. (Rom. 15:4)

LEAKY FLOATS ARE no fun in the pool. As long as the float holds some air, kids will try to make it work—but when the air leaks out completely, so does the fun. Tough times poke holes in your heart, and hope leaks out.

Can a leaky heart be refilled with hope? Yes, but it must be *true* hope that is sourced in our living God.

In the Bible, God has provided many wonderful records of his strength and his character. He has also provided many amazing promises that Christians can count on. Paul wrote today's verse as he looked back at the Old Testament. According to what Paul says in Romans, Bible stories are not just for Sunday school classes or for Bible trivia games—they were written "for our instruction" and so that you might be encouraged. Their goal is to refocus your hope by reminding you of the greatness of God.

Think of a familiar Bible story like that of David and Goliath. The Philistines were fiercely oppressing Israel. Their supersized champion, Goliath, issued a challenge to the armies of Israel— winner take all. King Saul and the rest of the Israelites shook in their sandals before young David rose to the challenge. The Israelites were outmatched in size, strength, experience, and weaponry. Although their human resources were small, David had a heart full of hope in God. He killed Goliath with a sling and a stone and Goliath's own sword.

Or think of the story of Moses returning to Egypt to challenge Pharaoh to let God's people go from slavery. Humanly speaking, this was a hopeless proposition, but Moses obeyed God. He believed God. He hoped in God's promises. He wasn't afraid of Pharaoh's anger, because he saw him who was invisible (see Heb. 11:27).

The Christian's God today is the same as David's and Moses's God. The stories in Scripture demonstrate that hope in God is solid, true, real, and effective. Those who hope in God can be used by him to do impossible things. If God was faithful to David and Moses, he will be faithful to you too. You have the exact same God, the God of the Bible.

Reflect: Think of how God kept his promises to people in history such as Abraham and Sarah (see Gen. 17). Their son Isaac was born after twenty-five long years (see Gen. 21). Isaac married Rebekah, and after twenty years, she had Jacob and Esau (see Gen. 25). Does God's promise-keeping in the past inspire hope now?

Reflect: Nearly one thousand years after David, Jesus Christ was born in King David's line (see Matt. 1:1–17). How does knowing this finale to the Old Testament stories strengthen your faith?

Act: Think about three favorite Old Testament stories. Read them in their context. List specific ways that each provides hope for your situation.

DAY 11

God Is for You

He who did not spare his own Son but gave him up for us all,
how will he not also with him graciously give us all things?
Who shall bring any charge against God's elect? It is God who
justifies. Who is to condemn? Christ Jesus is the one who died—
more than that, who was raised—who is at the right hand of
God, who indeed is interceding for us. (Rom. 8:32–34)

AN UNASSUMING MAN walks up and asks to join your soccer
game in the park. Because you are being trounced and humili-
ated, you hardly take notice. But as he approaches, you recognize
that your new teammate is Lionel Messi, one of the greatest soccer players in the world. Everything about your game is about to
change because Messi is on your side.

In hard times, it is easy to lose sight of God. You fixate on
the details of your difficult circumstances and desperately grasp
for human solutions to your problems. You think like a practical
atheist, one who claims to believe in God but lives as though he
doesn't exist: "Certainly God is there, but I need to pay this bill
this week" or "God is there, but I need another procedure to give
me a better result" or "I'm sure God is there, but if that job doesn't
come through, our family will not have health coverage." When
pressed, you do not believe God is actively working in your hard
situation.

One of the sweetest sentences in the Bible is found in
Romans 8: "We know that for those who love God all things
work together for good, for those who are called according to
his purpose" (v. 28). God is superintending the good, bad, and
ugly events of life to bring about his glory and the good of his
people. The rest of Romans 8 makes the point that God is for

his people. Christian hope is not merely that God will ultimately swing bad things around in eternity—Christians can take heart today because God is working *for them*.

God has all power, all knowledge, all wisdom, and he is everywhere all of the time. He cannot be stopped. Even when he allows evil to prevail briefly, he is overriding its purposes and accomplishing something far better.

The logic of Romans 8 is inspiring. "What then shall we say to these things? If God is for us, who can be against us? He who did not spare his own Son but gave him up for us all, how will he not also with him graciously give us all things?" (vv. 31–32). To be a Christian means trusting in the person and work of the Lord Jesus Christ. God loved you and sent his beloved Son to suffer and die upon the cross and to be raised from the dead on the third day. If God loved you enough to crush the Lord Jesus Christ for you when you were in your sin, obviously he continues to love you now that you are his child.

Hope knows that God is present, God loves you, and God is working for you. That kind of knowledge changes the game.

Reflect: The end of Romans 8 powerfully affirms God's love for his children (see vv. 38–39). Are you looking only at your hopeless circumstances? Widen your gaze to include the God who loves you and is for you.

Act: As you bring your burdens to the Lord in prayer, thank him that he is for you. Repeatedly reminding yourself of that single truth will strengthen your muscle of hope.

DAY 12

God Delights in the Hopeful

His delight is not in the strength of the horse, nor his pleasure in the legs of a man, but the LORD takes pleasure in those who fear him, in those who hope in his steadfast love. (Ps. 147:10–11)

IF YOU HAD a million dollars in your briefcase, would you be impressed by a man dancing around because he found a quarter? God has much more than a million dollars. In fact, all things ultimately come from his bounty.

Because God owns such remarkable resources, resourceful people fail to impress him. He does not delight in a horse's or a man's strength. Instead, we learn in today's verses that God's pleasure is in those who fear him and in those who hope in his steadfast love.

Does this describe you? This fear means honoring and revering the Lord. *Fear* of the Lord and *hope* in his love are a powerful combination. God likes it when his creatures recognize their neediness and then look to him for support.

It seems impossible to believe that God is truly pleased with those who fear him and who hope in his steadfast love. Those experiencing painful trials often acknowledge that their best hope efforts are mixed with worry, self-pity, and unbelieving thoughts. Perhaps God could be happy with a Christian who perfectly puts pure hope in him, but no one actually qualifies. Some teachers suggest that passages like Psalm 147:10–11 exist only to remind those in trials of their unworthiness and to point them to their Savior so at least they can be forgiven failures.

I don't think so. It is true that all people sin and fall short of God's standards (see Rom. 3:23) and that after someone trusts in Jesus, he or she is declared righteous and adopted into God's family (see Rom. 6:23; 8:14–17). But just as earthly parents love their children and are pleased with their imperfect efforts to obey, God chooses to be pleased when his children try to respect him and to hope in him.

Do you want to please God? You can, even in hardship: Stop staring at your circumstances and counting on human resources. God is not impressed by your little quarter. Look to God. He is the right object of your hope. And in spite of your wavering hope, he will take special delight in your efforts to hope in him.

Reflect: The Lord is mindful that you are but dust (see Ps. 103:14). He knows all about your fickle heart. He still desires to be your hope. Are you willing to put your hope in him?

Act: Form this outline into a prayer of your own: (1) Praise God for his love, knowledge, and power. (2) Confess your lack of adequate resources. (3) Ask for courage to hope in him. (4) Express your desire to please him.

DAY 13

God Is Sovereign

*"As for you, you meant evil against me, but God meant
it for good, to bring it about that many people should
be kept alive, as they are today." (Gen. 50:20)*

HOW MANY BAD days in a row can you take before quitting?
God wants you to honor him even when life is tough, but what
about when life is tough for a really long time? Remember Joseph's
story in the Bible. How many bad days did Joseph endure?

Joseph went from being his father's favorite son to being
thrown in a pit and sold to traveling traders. We can imagine Joseph
responded well to the immediate crisis: Perhaps he was still able to
wonder with faith how God would get glory in his terrible situation.
Joseph, seventeen years old and full of spiritual and physical energy,
may have thought, "Surely this circumstance will turn around soon."

Potiphar, an Egyptian captain, purchased the young Israelite
man, and things finally began to look up. Potiphar noticed Joseph's
faithful service and entrusted him with his household. "See, God
still sees me. It won't be long before I'm back at home," Joseph
may have thought. But along came Potiphar's wife with her lust.
She falsely accused Joseph, who found himself thrown into prison.

Could Joseph still hope in God after being slandered and mis-
treated? Apparently so. He served God faithfully in prison, and
again he was noticed and put in charge of the jail. But as the hard
years passed, Joseph's hope must have wobbled from time to time.

Joseph interpreted the dreams of two fellow prisoners: Pharaoh's baker would be executed, but Pharaoh's cupbearer would
be restored to his position. Hope was reborn when the cupbearer
promised to tell Pharaoh about Joseph's plight. But the cupbearer
forgot Joseph. If Joseph was marking each day on his cell wall, he

would have slashed seven hundred and thirty more marks before Pharaoh had dreams that required interpretation.

Joseph was thirty years old when they dragged him out of the pit and set him before Pharaoh. He spent his entire twenties in Egypt as either a slave or a prisoner. He had thirteen years' worth of bad days.

God enabled Joseph to interpret Pharaoh's dreams and to plan for the upcoming famine. Joseph was elevated to a powerful position, and his preparations saved Egypt, plus multitudes in the surrounding nations—including Joseph's own family.

God was working out a wonderful plan all along, and Joseph eventually realized it. When his brothers begged for his mercy after their father died, Joseph said, "Do not fear, for am I in the place of God? As for you, you meant evil against me, but God meant it for good, to bring it about that many people should be kept alive, as they are today. So do not fear; I will provide for you and your little ones" (Gen. 50:19–21).

Don't give up. God is at work. He is wise, big, powerful, faithful, and loving. He knows all about your situation. All your bad days are before him. One day (it may be in heaven), you will understand too, as God reveals what he was accomplishing. But, until that day, trust what you know about God's character. Consider Joseph. Keep hoping.

Reflect: How is it possible to maintain hope, even if you're in a trial that is lasting a long time? You must keep remembering God.

Act: Do whatever it takes to stay mindful of God. Read your Bible. Pray. Memorize hope-giving verses such as Genesis 50:20. Listen to Christian music with lyrics extolling God's greatness. Spend time with Christians who say true things about God.

DAY 14

God's Resurrection Power Brings Hope

We do not want you to be unaware . . . of the affliction we experienced in Asia. For we were so utterly burdened beyond our strength that we despaired of life itself. Indeed, we felt that we had received the sentence of death. But that was to make us rely not on ourselves but on God who raises the dead. He delivered us from such a deadly peril, and he will deliver us. On him we have set our hope that he will deliver us again. (2 Cor. 1:8–10)

SOMETIMES THE APOSTLE Paul seems superhuman. He can be thrown in jail and sing songs, survive earthquakes, and lead the jailer to Christ. He can be anticipating a life-or-death verdict from Caesar but still rejoicing that Caesar's guards have heard the gospel.

But Paul was not superhuman. He had bad days when he cracked under the pressure and lost hope. The Corinthians seem to have been aware of one of Paul's extreme trials but not of his despair. Paul doesn't describe the specifics of his difficult situation. Instead, he uses an assortment of superlatives to convey his deep distress. He states it just the way it was. He felt so utterly burdened that he was beyond his strength. His anxiety was so alarming that he despaired of life itself. The root of Paul's descriptive word *despaired* means "no way out." The prison door didn't have a key. It was over. His life seemed to be hanging by a thread. The verb tenses indicate these feelings were ongoing, not momentary. How long? We don't know. But it sounds awful.

Paul's load surpassed his physical limits and exhausted his emotional limits. It felt beyond his spiritual limits as well. Do you feel like this, overwhelmed and exhausted with no hope of relief?

Looking back, Paul saw God sovereignly working during that massive trial. God was teaching Paul not to rely upon himself but to rely on God, who, as Paul added, raises the dead. God has allowed you to experience your terrible trial. If he were a weak and foolish God, you would have no hope at all. But just as Paul realized, he is the God of resurrection power.

God raised Paul out of the depths of his despair, and Paul declared that God was the basis of his hope (see 2 Cor. 1:10). Confidence in such a faithful, powerful, wise, and loving God reinvigorated his weakened heart.

Reflect: God's resurrection power offers hope: he can raise you up, no matter if you are physically, emotionally, financially, or even spiritually dead.

Act: Paul's hope revived as he considered what God was accomplishing in his massive trial. Journal about your problems, but include biblical truths about God in and around your problems. Let a trusted friend read your entry, and pray together for endurance and hope in God amidst the trial.

DAY 15

God Is More Gracious Than You Can Imagine

He prayed to him, and God was moved by his entreaty and heard his plea and brought him again to Jerusalem into his kingdom. Then Manasseh knew that the LORD was God. (2 Chron. 33:13)

HAVE YOU BLOWN it so badly that you wonder if there's hope for a fresh start? At least one man in the Bible was far worse than you: if there was hope for him, there is hope for you too.

Because of Solomon's idolatry, God split the kingdom of Israel into two—Israel and Judah. In Judah's 350 years, eight rulers did what was right before God. Hezekiah was one of Judah's best kings, but his example failed to impress his son Manasseh.

Hezekiah died when his son was twelve, and Manasseh became king for the next fifty-five years. The Bible says he "did what was evil in the sight of the LORD" (2 Kings 21:2). Hezekiah destroyed pagan shrines in the country, but Manasseh rebuilt them and even made God's temple into a pagan shrine. His wickedness reached new heights as he sacrificed his sons in fire to the false god Molech. The Bible says Manasseh used fortune-tellers, wizards, and sorcery. He sinned in the face of God and led the nation to rebel as well. The Bible says that Judah's sins against God were worse than those of the surrounding pagan nations.

When the king of Assyria assaulted Judah, captured Manasseh, and took him to Babylon with hooks and chains, amazingly the story did not end there.

In Babylon, Manasseh repented.

This was no jailhouse religion. Manasseh humbled himself and sought God's forgiveness, and the Bible says God heard his prayer. God forgave Manasseh for his sin and let him return to Jerusalem. Manasseh's subsequent lifestyle proved his true heart change. He cleaned up the temple and undid the idolatry in Judah that he had promoted for so many years. He commanded the people to serve only the Lord.

God is holy and just. While he is patient, he does not tolerate wickedness forever. How is it right for God to forgive Manasseh when he was so evil? Where is justice in this story? God could forgive Manasseh because of what God would do to Jesus some 650 years later. All the wrath Manasseh deserved, God poured out on Jesus. All the punishment for the most wicked king of Judah was inflicted on the most righteous King of Judah. God would punish Jesus so he could offer Manasseh grace and still be righteous

Have you ever thought that Jesus died for some sins but that there must be a limit on the cross's capacity? Of course the devil would whisper to you that your sins have exceeded the limits of God's mercy. The hope in Manasseh's story is that God is more gracious than you can imagine and the cross is massively effective: you can be forgiven too!

Reflect: Tell the Lord what is in your heart. Confess your massive sin. Repent. Call upon the Lord for the same kind of mercy that Manasseh received. Are you willing to turn to the Lord today? If there is hope for Manasseh, there is hope for you and me.

Act: Read Manasseh's story in 2 Kings 21 and 2 Chronicles 33. Look for the depths of his sin and the heights of God's grace.

DAY 16

God Himself Will Get Us Through

Keep your life free from love of money, and be content with what you have, for he has said, "I will never leave you nor forsake you." (Heb. 13:5)

A MISSION REQUIRES resources. To have a hopeful attitude for the assignments God has given, you must remember the resources that God will provide. The essential resource you have is God's presence with you. An old saying goes, "God and me make a majority." That is right. Can you imagine any righteous task you could not accomplish with God working beside you? What army could stand before you and God? What friend are you scared to engage when God is present and working?

Can you truly expect the living God to walk with you through a challenging situation? You can: throughout the Bible, God repeatedly promises his presence to motivate his servants to accomplish impossibly difficult tasks.

When Moses was stuttering at the thought of appealing to Pharaoh, God said that he would be with Moses's mouth and teach it what to say. Moses had a hard task from God, but God was his resource to accomplish it.

God called Gideon to lead the people of Israel against the Midianite army. What hope did Gideon and his tiny army of thirty-two thousand oppressed Israelites have of defeating such a fierce foe? God's strategy to help Gideon was to first reduce his army by twenty-two thousand men who were afraid to fight and then to get rid of 9,700 more. Gideon had to finish the job with three hundred men. Three hundred men, plus God. God routed the entire Midianite army.

When Jesus told his followers to make disciples of all the people groups, could Christians have hope of real success?

Sometimes spiritual conversations with friends are hard; how could the followers of Jesus evangelize the world? Our hope is in the promise at the end of the Great Commission: "Behold, I am with you always, to the end of the age" (Matt. 28:20).

In Hebrews 13, God calls Christians to purity (see v. 4) and contentment (see v. 5) while the whole world tempts them to sin: Have a sexually immoral and adulterous relationship. Idolize money so you can get what you want. Maybe you can even buy contentment? But believers must look to God for hope. God promised his presence to each Christian: "For he has said, 'I will never leave you nor forsake you.' So we can confidently say, 'The Lord is my helper; I will not fear; what can man do to me?'" (vv. 5–6).

You can have hope today because God himself is your resource to complete all the tasks he has given you. He is with you.

In the beloved Twenty-Third Psalm, King David imagines himself as a helpless lamb. But that helpless lamb is not hopeless, because God is the lamb's Shepherd. God's sheep are always well cared for. In the midst of the song, the sweetest word of encouragement comes. "Even though I walk through the valley of the shadow of death, I will fear no evil, for you are with me; your rod and your staff, they comfort me" (v. 4).

Reflect: Have you been thinking about your daily tasks like a practical atheist? Certainly, you believe in God, but have you been thinking about God's presence with you as you ponder the missions God has given you?

Act: Emphasize each one of those true words of the promise in Psalm 23:4 and feel waves of hope wash over your heart. He is with you. He is with you. He is with you. He is with you.

DAY 17

Our Omnipotent God Cares

The angel [Gabriel] answered her, . . . "For nothing will be impossible with God." And Mary said, "Behold, I am the servant of the Lord; let it be to me according to your word." (Luke 1:35, 37–38)

MY FRIEND ONCE commented on the incredible popularity of a TV preacher. He suggested that the preacher's popularity comes from his big smile and positive message in welcome contrast to our ultra-negative world.

Our world assaults us with negativity. The media blares on about the bad economy, rumors of wars, and extreme political ideas. Some people have no relationships; others endure bad ones that they wish they didn't have. Kids aren't living up to their parents' wishes. Families strain like rubber bands stretched tight for too long. Doctors also give negative news. As people age, they fall apart. Some battle new bulges, and others battle for their lives.

Such relentless pounding crushes hearts and warps perspectives. When your family, your friends, and the media beat you down day after day, it sucks the life from your soul. You start to feel dead inside. Hollow hearts lead to complaining mouths, anger, fighting, disappointment, and much more, which extend negativity's reach. Smiles and platitudes are not enough to overcome this negative world.

The Christmas hymn "O Holy Night" contains a significant phrase that captures the emotional effect of a heart filled with hope: the "thrill of hope." Even when all seems negative, you can still feel hope's thrill. You can have joy, optimism, energy, thrill, endurance, and a conviction that the future will be good.

How? Think of the amazing message that the angel Gabriel brought to Mary: she would bear a child—God's Son. How in the world could a young virgin girl even become pregnant, much less carry the Son of God to full term? Gabriel's answer was clear: "Nothing will be impossible with God" (Luke 1:37).

Without God, the fallen world really is a dark place. If you have a big smile and a positive attitude, you might flicker a little light, but negativity quickly snuffs it out.

The all-powerful God exists, and he cares for you. He hears and answers prayers. If all you can do is leave a problem in God's hands, you are leaving it in the best possible hands. He has the power to pull off the impossible.

Reflect: Identify some of the world's negativity that extinguishes your hope.

Act: Personalize this prayer: "You are a mighty God, absolutely sovereign. Forgive me for doubting your strength in this dark world. My strength is small, and my problems loom large, but you are so much stronger. Fill me with faith. Remind me of the clear statements of your sovereignty and the stories showcasing your strength. You allowed my troubles and are working through them. Everything sometimes seems so negative. But as I think about you, my massive problems seem small. I bow before your throne in humility and hope. Amen."

DAY 18

The Lord Is Worth the Wait

*For God alone, O my soul, wait in silence, for
my hope is from him. (Ps. 62:5)*

WAITING AROUND IS not fun—especially if your phone battery is dead. It can seem like years of your life have been spent in the doctor's office, the Department of Driver Services, theme park lines, and rush hour traffic.

The return of the Lord Jesus is definite, but it hasn't happened yet. And so Christians wait. We are confident in God's character and promises, but our hope requires endurance: "If we hope for what we do not see, we wait for it with patience" (Rom. 8:25). One psalmist compares a believer hoping in God to the watchman waiting at his post with tiptoed expectation as he looks for the first rays of dawn (see Ps. 130:5–6). Other psalms also describe our waiting:

- "Wait for the LORD; be strong, and let your heart take courage; wait for the LORD!" (Ps. 27:14)
- "Be still before the LORD and wait patiently for him; fret not yourself over the one who prospers in his way, over the man who carries out evil devices!" (Ps. 37:7)
- "I will thank you forever, because you have done it. I will wait for your name, for it is good, in the presence of the godly." (Ps. 52:9)

The fact that we have to wait on God is not accidental. It is not a delay. He designs times of waiting, using them to build our patience and to strengthen our hope. When God's children patiently expect him to bring the help they need, it shows God that they recognize their dependence on him and trust him to come through.

God's timing also has purposes beyond you. Have you considered God may be delaying the answer to your prayer so that your testimony of waiting (prolonging your active hope) on him can help someone else who is watching?

Although you don't have access to God's calendar, you can know his heart as revealed in his Word. Your hope for God's good work in future events is just as sure as all God has accomplished in the past. Until God finishes his plan, you must wait for him—but you can know for certain that God's sovereign plan is good and wise. Waiting upon him is never in vain. He will always come through. He will deliver on every one of his promises. Your godly desires will be satisfied, according to God's perfect will and in God's perfect timing.

Reflect: Jeremiah declares, "The LORD is good to those who wait for him, to the soul who seeks him. It is good that one should wait quietly for the salvation of the LORD" (Lam. 3:25–26). Stop and consider if you believe these words. Is your attitude reflecting the hope of quiet waiting?

Act: Make a list of truths regarding God's character and God's sovereign plan for an issue for which you are awaiting a resolution. As you wait, thank him for the items on your list.

YOU CAN FACE
LIFE'S DIFFICULTIES
WITH HOPE

DAY 19

When You Feel Financial Pressure

"But seek first the kingdom of God and his righteousness,
and all these things will be added to you. Therefore do not be
anxious about tomorrow, for tomorrow will be anxious for itself.
Sufficient for the day is its own trouble." (Matt. 6:33–34)

MONTHS THAT END with more expenses than money can leave you miserable. You hate yourself for overspending and underplanning. You are angry that God allowed a budget buster to strike. You are ashamed that you let your family down. Or maybe things are okay, but you still worry that your money will run out.

Hope begins with thinking right thoughts about God. Don't become a practical atheist when you look into your wallet, bank account, and budget; God is there too. He cares about you and how you use your money. God owns all the world's resources and entrusts them to people to use on his behalf. God uses money in all kinds of ways. He tests you. He gives money and takes money away. He often shows you your heart through your bank statement.

God has many purposes in the financial ingredients of your specific recipe. Even if your messy money situation is your fault, he will graciously forgive you. Perhaps he is getting your attention through the pressure. Is your heart consumed with stuff instead of him?

God might not provide a quick fix. But you can still have hope. In Matthew 6, he has given wonderful promises to provide for the needs of his children. It is time to do some bird-watching. The Lord says that we are much more valuable to him than birds (see v. 26). Instead of fretting, the birds look for worms, and God supplies all that they need. He does the same for beautiful flowers that are here today and gone tomorrow (see vv. 28–30). Jesus calls people never to worry but to trust the same God who feeds the birds and clothes the lilies because he is their Father. He continues with this important heart reset: "But seek first the kingdom of God and his righteousness, and all these things will be added to you" (v. 33).

As you prioritize God and his ways in your heart, you can expect that he will care for your physical needs. Each day has plenty of trouble. Don't wonder and worry about your financial future. Look to God. He is the provider. He is your hope.

Reflect: If someone assessed your financial situation, what conclusions would they reach about your heart?

Act: If you are in a messy financial situation, humble yourself and go to a mature Christian for help and accountability. Together, come up with a plan.

Act: Hope comes from believing that God will keep his promises. Write Matthew 6:33–34 on an index card and memorize it. Intentionally work on believing it as you recite it.

DAY 20

When a Relationship Is Broken

Be kind to one another, tenderhearted, forgiving one
another, as God in Christ forgave you. (Eph. 4:32)

EVER SINCE SIN entered the world, relationships have been hard, and some relational wounds seem too deep to heal. Proverbs says, "A brother offended is more unyielding than a strong city, and quarreling is like the bars of a castle" (Prov. 18:19). If you are suffering because of a broken relationship, the Bible offers massive encouragement: If you and the estranged person want to please the Lord, God will unleash powerful resources to heal your relationship. Even if only one party is willing to reconcile, God still does miracles.

When Mark deserted Paul and Barnabas during their first missionary journey, Paul was keeping notes. When the second missionary trip rolled around, Barnabas wanted to bring Mark again, but Paul rejected the idea. The Bible uses strong words to describe their dispute: "Barnabas wanted to take with them John called Mark. But Paul thought best not to take with them one who had *withdrawn* from them in Pamphylia and had not gone with them to the work. And there arose a *sharp disagreement*, so that they *separated* from each other. Barnabas took Mark with him and sailed away to Cyprus, but Paul chose Silas and departed, having been commended by the brothers to the grace of the Lord" (Acts 15:37–40).

This separation is even worse in light of the close relationship that Paul and Barnabas previously shared. Barnabas took a chance on Paul, the former Christian-killer, and welcomed him into the Jerusalem churches. He later searched out Paul and brought him to Antioch for ministry training. Barnabas and Paul risked their lives together in pagan lands on the first missionary journey. And now this fight over integrity and forgiveness severed their relationship. The Bible doesn't discuss Barnabas after this, but it does mention Mark. When Paul sat in a cold Roman prison cell awaiting execution, he wrote a letter asking Mark to come and stay with him. Paul affirmed Mark's usefulness for service (see 2 Tim. 4:11).

Christians are called to "be kind to one another, tender-hearted, forgiving one another, as God in Christ forgave you" (Eph. 4:32). Such human forgiveness seems impossible unless you compare it to the quality and quantity of divine forgiveness we receive from the Lord. Offended friends can forgive each other because of the forgiveness of Jesus Christ. The hope lies in knowing that you have done what God asks of you. You do your part and then trust God to do the miracle (see Rom. 12:16–18). In a fallen world, your relationship may never be sorted out. But it might. God can do it. God delights in working miracles of grace. You can always trust God to do what is best.

Reflect: Do you feel hopeless about an estranged relationship? How might God do a miracle, in spite of how long things have been bad?

Act: List some blessings you can give to the one you are struggling with (see Rom. 12:14). Perhaps praying for the other person, writing a card, or giving a gift.

DAY 21

When Your Options Run Out

And that night the angel of the LORD went out and struck down 185,000 in the camp of the Assyrians. And when people arose early in the morning, behold, these were all dead bodies. (2 Kings 19:35)

HOPE CAN SURVIVE as long as there is a way out. The unemployed man tells himself sooner or later someone will hire him. The lonely single woman tries to believe that eventually someone will accept her. But what about when your options run out? Maybe a trial has lingered in your life far longer than you expected. At first you were optimistic because you knew it had to end eventually, but now you wonder. As your options run out, so does your hope.

It's hard to believe God can or will work when your options run out, but the Bible tells a story of God waiting until things seemed hopeless before enacting a massive rescue.

We met Hezekiah briefly in day 15. After Solomon's kingdom was divided in two, he was one of the few good kings who ruled the southern kingdom, Judah. During his reign, the terrifying world power Assyria wiped out the northern kingdom of Israel. A large, aggressive empire looming in your part of the world would be unsettling enough. But then Judah caught the evil giant's eye. Assyrian King Sennacherib marched his enormous army into Judah and started taking cities with ease. Soon only Jerusalem remained free. Sennacherib sent his messengers to taunt the people of Jerusalem to scare them into surrender. The messengers called the people foolish for listening to King Hezekiah when he said God would rescue them.

Hezekiah had nowhere to turn. The situation looked hopeless. The strongest nation in the world stood outside his walls, preparing to destroy what was left of God's people. It looked like the southern kingdom would be just another nation on the long list of Assyria's victims.

Hezekiah took Sennacherib's demand for surrender and "spread it before the LORD" (2 Kings 19:14). He prayed humbly, declaring that the gods of the nations Assyria destroyed were not gods but idols of wood and stone. Then he finished by praying, "So now, O LORD our God, save us, please, from his hand, that all the kingdoms of the earth may know that you, O LORD, are God alone" (v. 19).

God heard Hezekiah's desperate prayer and sent his prophet Isaiah to give a verbal reply. God promised to defeat Sennacherib, the most powerful ruler on earth (see 2 Kings 19:28).

Sennacherib and his expansive army lasted only eight more sentences. That night God sent his angel to kill 185,000 in the Assyrian camp. Can you imagine being a soldier of Jerusalem that morning? In one short night, you go from doomed and hopeless to completely victorious over the strongest nation in the world.

The same God is just as powerful today, and just like in Hezekiah's day, he responds to the humble prayers of his people. Whatever situation you are facing, even if you feel like there is no way out, consider how your trial is a platform for God to display his power and love for you. Pray to him humbly and wait for him to work.

Reflect: How hopeless did Hezekiah's situation seem just before the Lord answered his prayers?

Act: Take some time to write out a prayer of hope. Use Hezekiah's prayer as a guide (see 2 Kings 19:14–19), personalizing the details to fit your humanly impossible condition.

DAY 22

When Your World Collapses

The steadfast love of the LORD *never ceases; his mercies never come to an end; they are new every morning; great is your faithfulness. "The* LORD *is my portion," says my soul, "therefore I will hope in him." (Lam. 3:22–24)*

SOMETIMES LIFE'S PROBLEMS feel so enormous that the world's foundations seem to crack underfoot. Instead of missing a bill, it is financial ruin. Instead of a virus, it is a terminal disease. Instead of a troubled church member, it is a church split. How can you stay hopeful when your world collapses? Where can you go for hope when God is the one ultimately collapsing your world?

Jeremiah was God's prophet at the time of Judah's destruction. Over one hundred years before, God had sent the Assyrians to destroy the northern kingdom of Israel for their evil. Now the southern kingdom, Judah, was following the same sinful path. Jeremiah stood in their way and warned them to repent; instead, they ran him over, rejected his counsel, and literally tortured him for daring to challenge their rebellion. The Babylonians destroyed rebellious Jerusalem, smashing the walls, killing the people, and demolishing the temple. God's people were ejected from the promised land as the Babylonians forced the survivors into exile. Jeremiah is called "the weeping prophet" for good reason.

God is the ultimate source of destruction, but, as Jeremiah demonstrates in his lament over Jerusalem, God is also the ultimate source of hope.

Lamentations 3 records Jeremiah's desperate, authentic prayer to God. He cries, "Remember my affliction and my wanderings, the wormwood and the gall! My soul continually remembers it and is bowed down within me" (vv. 19–20).

Suddenly, a ray of hope blazes through his darkness, and he

recalls, "But this I call to mind, and therefore I have hope" (v. 21). Then come today's verses. Jeremiah realizes the larger reality of God's character, and his weak heart gains strength. He recalls God's never-ending, steadfast love and his ongoing mercies. God is not only faithful; his faithfulness is *great*. Because of this, Jeremiah then declares, "The LORD is my portion . . . therefore I will hope in him."

God was Jeremiah's portion, and this meant that Jeremiah and God were relationally connected. They had a true bond that would endure even the dark destruction of Israel. Jeremiah had grounds to maintain his hope in God. If you are a Christian, you are connected to Jesus Christ by faith. God is also your portion because of this sacred connection.

Jeremiah saw the smoke rising from the smoldering ruins of the temple. The smell of death filled his nostrils. But in spite of everything his senses screamed, Jeremiah knew that God was good and that his purposes were right. The prophet's job was to preach truth about God in spite of how he felt. "The LORD is good to those who wait for him, to the soul who seeks him. It is good that one should wait quietly for the salvation of the LORD" (vv. 25–26).

When your world is collapsing, God remains in ultimate control. That means God allows these collapses to occur in his wise master plan, though he could have stopped them. This certainly compels us to hope in God.

Reflect: What can make terrible circumstances feel so hopeless? How would you encourage a friend to have hope in such a circumstance?

Act: Pray about your circumstances like Jeremiah. He cried out for Judah to repent. They did not, and God brought devastation. As miserable as he was, Jeremiah went to God to find strengthening hope.

DAY 23

When Your Hopes Are Dashed

*And the crowds that went before him and that followed him were shouting,
"Hosanna to the Son of David! Blessed is he who comes in the name of
the Lord! Hosanna in the highest!" And when he entered Jerusalem, the
whole city was stirred up, saying, "Who is this?" (Matt. 21:9–10)*

IN THE MOVIE *Cars 2*, the arrogant race car Francesco quipped,
"To truly crush one's dream, you must first raise their hopes very
high." Losing feels worse when you had high hopes of winning.

When the Jews had no earthly hope of defeating the Romans,
they looked to the Scriptures. They read about past times when
God empowered his people to defeat their foes despite all odds,
like David against Goliath and Joshua at Jericho. They also read
about the Messiah coming in the future, and this energized their
expectations.

Throughout the Old Testament, messianic predictions devel-
oped but remained shadowy and indistinct. The people knew the
Messiah would be born from King David's line in Bethlehem.
They knew he would do miracles and preach God's truth like no
other. They knew he would reign over and judge God's enemies.
How could this not be about the Romans?

By the time Jesus entered the historical scene, all these hopes
were burning like wildfire. In today's verses from Matthew 21,
Jesus comes to Jerusalem riding on a donkey. The people pour
out of the city to meet him. They bring out branches and shout,
"Hosanna to the Son of David" (v. 9). "The Son of David" is a
reference to the Messiah, who comes from David's line. Hosanna
means "Lord save us." All their hopes erupt into confident expectations. Their hopes are raised very high!

But then their hopes are dashed to pieces. Jesus isn't going to defeat the Romans. He cleanses the temple's spiritual corruption (see Matt. 21:12–17), disputes with the religious leaders (see Matt. 21:23–24), and affirms that taxes should be rendered to Caesar (see Matt. 22:15–22). The people's dashed expectations become bitter cries for Jesus's crucifixion later that same week.

Most of the Jews' hopes had been hollow. But as Jesus died on the cross, God poured out his wrath on Jesus in the place of sinners. God was making way for a much greater liberation than anyone in Israel imagined. Three days later, God raised Jesus from the grave. In conquering death, Christ gives us—those who have repented and trusted in Jesus—eternal life in him.

If Jesus had relieved Israel from Roman rule, how many years would a typical Jew have benefited? How long has anyone who trusts Christ for salvation benefited (so far) from relief from God's wrath? A few happier years on earth are no replacement for forever in heaven. Sometimes dashed hopes are misplaced hopes.

Reflect: Take inventory of your despair. Have you been hoping in the wrong objects? Which expectations should you shift to have more ground for true hope?

Act: Talk with a mature Christian friend about the basis for your hope.

DAY 24

When You Are Struggling with Sin

For we do not wrestle against flesh and blood, but against the rulers, against the authorities, against the cosmic powers over this present darkness, against the spiritual forces of evil in the heavenly places. (Eph. 6:12)

IMMEDIATELY AFTER successfully tempting a Christian to sin, the devil changes tactics and slyly asks, "If you are a real Christian, why do you still struggle with so much sin?" He does jujitsu, using the opponent's body weight against them. If Satan catches you leaning in, he yanks you forward with more temptations. But if you pull back after sinning, he shoves you with accusations.

Ironically, the Bible's teaching that Christians continually struggle with sin can increase hope. You are not alone. You are not strange. If you battle tempting thoughts, regularly repent, and sometimes have mud on your feet, you are a normal Christian.

Paul describes the Christian life as an internal war: "The desires of the flesh are against the Spirit, and the desires of the Spirit are against the flesh, for these are opposed to each other, to keep you from doing the things you want to do" (Gal. 5:17). Even though Christians are forgiven and have new desires and abilities to honor God, the remnants of their flesh will try to pull them back to their old ways throughout their entire lives.

The gospel reminds Christians that their right standing before God never depends upon personal performance. Paul highlights the gospel in his instruction about spiritual warfare in Ephesians 6. The believer fights sin and temptation with gospel hope. As Paul describes the Christian's protection in terms of a Roman soldier's armor, he calls his readers to put on the belt of truth, the helmet of salvation, the breastplate of righteousness, and gospel shoes (see vv. 14–17). Even the shield is faith—believing all that

God says is true (see v. 16). The only offensive weapon Christians have is a sword: the sword of the Spirit, which is the Word of God (see v. 17).

As the devil does his jujitsu, remember Jesus and the cross, and believe the truth that God says about you. When the devil shoves with accusations, believe that your righteousness is a gift that Jesus Christ gave to you. Allow that great news to comfort and inspire you to honor God.

God puts his children on a path to Christlikeness. The master sculptor chips away all the jagged imperfections to create a work of art. Your battles with sin, even the ones you lose, are part of his master plan (see Rom. 8:28–30). While God is never the author of sin, he powerfully overrules the devil's intentions to accomplish his greater goals.

Don't be surprised by your continuing struggles with sin. You are actually far worse than you realize, but your ultimate righteousness is found in Christ and is not sustained by your performance. God knows all about your spiritual weaknesses. You are making real progress in your fight against sin, in spite of how things may seem. God is working in your life. He will not stop working until the job is complete. He won't let your burdens knock you out for the count. He will not. He has promised.

Reflect: We can't distinguish whether attacks are from the devil or our own flesh. Both spiritual enemies work in the same ways and are defeated by your gospel armor. How can thinking rightly about the gospel be a primary means of spiritual warfare?

Act: List the pieces of the believer's armor in Ephesians 6:10–18. Write ways the gospel relates to each one and how to use each piece in your spiritual battles.

DAY 25

When You Feel
Abandoned by God

*I am weary with my moaning; every night I flood my bed with
tears; I drench my couch with my weeping. My eye wastes away
because of grief; it grows weak because of all my foes. (Ps. 6:6–7)*

FOR THREE THOUSAND YEARS, the Psalms have encouraged God's people. As David expressed his heart, the Holy Spirit
was inspiring the king to feel what he felt and to write what he
wrote. As you read the Psalms, the Holy Spirit energizes you to
connect with the tragedies and triumphs of the sacred songs, even
when your circumstances differ. As David and the other writers
grasp for God in their most intense situations, you can imitate
their efforts and find the same God.

Consider this restatement of Psalm 6. Can you connect with
David to find hope in your own unique situation?

"O Lord, you have every reason to be furious at me. Because
your eyes see my heart's thoughts and motives, you know I blew
it and deserve your wrath. Your anger is burning. I'm asking that
you would be merciful and stop the painful discipline.

"I'm a mess. I feel my sin and my terrible circumstances all the
way down to my bones. Be gracious to me. Please heal me. I have
trouble trembling within my soul. It seems like you are far away.
I don't know how much longer I can hang on.

"God, please look at me. Save me. I know I don't deserve your
mercy. But I also know that your love is so loyal that you are kind
even when your people don't deserve anything good. Please think
about your great love more than you think about what I've earned.

"I could die. When my body is in the grave, I won't make any noise. There will be no songs of thanks from my dead lips. There will be no breath to turn into remembrances of you. Please save me before I die, so I can use my mouth to praise you.

"Things are so hard for me that I am tired of moaning. I'm lying in puddles of tears in my bed. Can eyes melt from tears? If so, mine are close to wasting away. Everyone seems against me, and the grief is too much to bear.

"But there is hope! Listen up, you workers of wickedness—you'd better go. The Lord has heard me! My weeping has not been in vain. Let my opponents beware. God is about to respond to how you have treated me. You should run.

"God cares for even me in my pathetic state. He is about to turn my world around.

"My enemies seemed to have their way with me. They have boasted proudly of their victory over me. That is about to change. God will take their proud faces and smash them into the ground. Their mocking songs will become songs of shame and trouble. I have been defeated for a long time. All that will change when God moves in. In one moment, they will be turned back—their honor will turn to shame."

Reflect: Can you relate to David's desperation? I hope you can also relate to David's attempts to get to God. He felt spiritually isolated. David appealed to God's love and mercy instead of his own personal worthiness. Even if you don't deserve his mercy and love, you can still hope in God.

Act: Carefully compare Psalm 6 with the restatement above. Try writing your own restatement of Psalm 6.

DAY 26

When You Wrestle with Despair

*Why are you cast down, O my soul, and why are you in
turmoil within me? Hope in God; for I shall again praise
him, my salvation and my God. (Ps. 42:5–6)*

THE PSALMS SPEAK realistically about tough situations, with
the inspired writers venting their emotions on full display. God
often shows up in unexpected ways—not every psalm ends with
"happily ever after." Authentic descriptions of problems show
you can trust in God's prescriptions.

One of the instructions in God's Word says that in times of
deep despair, when everything is going wrong, you should stop
giving in to negative voices and instead command yourself to
hope in God.

We see this in Psalms 42 and 43, where the psalmist repeats
this accusatory question: "Why are you cast down, O my soul,
and why are you in turmoil within me?" (Ps. 42:5, 11; 43:5). And
each time, he repeats word for word a command to hope: "Hope
in God; for I shall again praise him, my salvation and my God"
(Ps. 42:5–6, 11; 43:5).

This is an important prescription for despair.

The psalm's author reveals his deep hopelessness in many
ways, including feelings of abandonment. Many people put the
first verses of Psalm 42 in sweet songs and on pretty posters: "As a
deer pants for flowing streams, so pants my soul for you, O God.
My soul thirsts for God, for the living God" (vv. 1–2). The visual
is of a dehydrated deer dying in the woods, desperate to touch his
wooden tongue to water. This is how the psalmist describes his
desperate relationship with God.

His only food has been hot, salty tears. People insult his

distance from God (see v. 10). Memories of former times with God mock his present loneliness (see vv. 3–4). He feels utterly forsaken, like God has forgotten him (see v. 9).

When you feel alone, what do you do? You know God must be the answer, but honestly, his absence is a big part of the problem. In Psalm 42, adversaries start directing the psalmist to turn against God, but that isn't right.

Here is where the author of the psalm brings his surprising solution: Tell yourself the truth about God. Hope in God. In spite of how far away the Lord seems to be, he is with you under your pile of problems.

You feel hopeless, helpless, and abandoned by God. Although that is how you feel, those feelings aren't accurate. They are not the whole story. Don't give in to them! Instead, speak truth to your soul—hope in God! Lift your eyes to heaven. He is worthy of your praise. He is your God.

Get your ears away from the voices of fake friends and of your own weakened heart. Remember what is true about God. Your fallen, fickle feelings may let you down, but God will not.

In a world plagued by sinfulness, you cannot always trust your heart. When your heart tells you wrong things about God and your dark circumstances, you must tell yourself the truth from Scripture. The end of this story *will* result in praises to him.

Reflect: Are your negative thoughts on a continual loop? Stop! Insert God into your thinking now.

Act: Write examples of what you have been telling yourself. Next to each negative thought, write a God-centered replacement thought. Hoping in God includes using self-control to think these new thoughts instead of the negative ones when they try to return.

DAY 27

When a Believing Loved One Dies

But we do not want you to be uninformed, brothers,
about those who are asleep, that you may not grieve as
others do who have no hope. (1 Thess. 4:13)

DEATH IS SO final and ugly that Jake fought to sort out his sad thoughts about his friend Christopher. Even though Christopher didn't suffer much pain before dying, he was still dead. Jake could never speak to Christopher again on this earth. Their plans for a trip together weren't just on hold; they were over. Christopher's contagious laughter was already fading from Jake's memory. Jake knew he lost a huge source of comfort, encouragement, and advice.

Jake thought death was the most hopeless condition possible. But the Bible says hope is possible after someone has died. The apostle Paul reminds us in today's verse, as Christians, we don't have to grieve as those who have no hope. That's how the world grieves because the world sees death as final. Both Christopher and Jake belong to God, so Jake actually has more reason for hope than he realizes.

Death ended Christopher's existence on earth, and his spirit is temporarily separated from his dead body. A Christian who dies is with the Lord. Jesus said to the criminal on the cross, "Truly, I say to you, today you will be with me in paradise" (Luke 23:43). Jesus is now in paradise, and Christians who die join Jesus there. So, yes, Christopher is in a better place—with Jesus. But there is even more hope for Jake than that.

When Jesus comes back, the dead in Christ will rise. As Jesus comes down from heaven with a trumpet blast, Christopher will come with him (see 1 Thess. 4:16). The Lord will instantaneously renew Christopher's physical body. The Lord will reunite Christopher's detached spirit with his renewed body. Christopher and every believer who has died will join the Lord's entourage and celebration triumph as he returns to earth.

At that point, the Jakes left in the world will be changed on the spot and launch into the sky to join this glorious assembly in the clouds (see 1 Thess. 4:15, 17). Christians alive when Jesus returns will experience the same transformation that Christopher and those who have already died will experience, without having to go through the detachment of death.

Jake and Christopher will then always be with the Lord. They will be with each other as well, and their friendship can continue. Jake will still be Jake, and Christopher will still be Christopher. But they will also be better. They will never be tempted to sin against each other again. There will never be a day that one has to follow up with the other, confessing sin and asking forgiveness.

None of these wonderful truths remove Jake's sadness. Jake still feels the fog of grief over the loss of Christopher. Right now, he can't see Christopher or talk to him. He feels the massive void. But within Jake's sad heart, there can also be real hope. Jake looks forward to the day when Christ returns, the dead in Christ will rise, and those still alive will also join Jesus!

Reflect: This life is short next to eternity. Everyone who lives will see loved ones pass away. Why is it so important to arm yourself ahead of time with the truth so you can grieve with hope?

Act: Think of ways to graciously encourage a grieving friend about the death of a fellow believer at the funeral, a week later, and a few months later. If you are not sure how best to do this, get advice from a mature Christian friend.

HOPE IN THE END

DAY 28

Because He Lives

If in Christ we have hope in this life only, we are of all people most to be pitied. But in fact Christ has been raised from the dead, the firstfruits of those who have fallen asleep. (1 Cor. 15:19–20)

WE SAW IN DAY 23 that under the oppressive reign of the Roman empire, Jews longed for the promised Messiah to liberate the promised land. When Jesus began his ministry, myriads of Jews thought he was that expected Christ. With his amazing words and works, he seemed to ride the tidal wave of their expectations. When he was tortured and executed upon the cross, though, their hopes were wrecked.

Then, on the first day of the week, some of the women reported to the disciples that Jesus's tomb was empty. Two of Jesus's followers heard these words and started sprinting to the tomb. Their minds raced as they ran through the gates of Jerusalem toward the place Jesus's body had been laid. They confirmed that the tomb was empty, but the light had still not penetrated the darkness in their minds.

Later that day, Jesus appeared to his followers in a locked room. As bright light drives darkness away, hope pushed out the darkness in their hearts. Questions remained, but hope swelled. The flicker intensified into a flame and then spread into a fire of faith and living hope.

The resurrection of Jesus had validated all his words and works. He truly is the Christ. His resurrection also proved that there is more to life than life—there is a judgment and an eternity in a real heaven or a real hell.

If the story had ended with Jesus's death, Paul writes, those who trust in him would be the world's most pitiful people. But a hope better than all earthly hopes had risen with the sun on the third day. As Peter later wrote, "[God] has caused us to be born again to a living hope through the resurrection of Jesus Christ from the dead" (1 Peter 1:3).

Hope was still necessary for the early Christians, and it is necessary for you. You aren't in heaven with Christ yet, but your expectations can be strong. All that Jesus promised thus far has come to pass. He proved himself by the resurrection. Now you await the finale, when you will see and experience all that Jesus described.

Darkness may appear to be prevailing in the world. It may seem to be prevailing in your life. But if you are a Christian, you don't have hope for *this life only*—you have ultimate hope. This tiny lifetime will be swallowed up in eternity. Because Jesus lives, you will live. You will be resurrected to eternal life just as he was.

Reflect: In what ways does Jesus's resurrection inspire hope in your specific circumstances?

Act: Challenge a Christian friend to think more carefully about the hope-filled implications of the resurrection. First, discuss the pitiful situation it would be if Christ had not been raised. Then, celebrate together several of the ways your future is different because Christ has been raised.

DAY 29

The Blessed Hope
of Christ's Return

*For the grace of God has appeared, bringing salvation for all
people, training us to renounce ungodliness and worldly passions,
and to live self-controlled, upright, and godly lives in the present age,
waiting for our blessed hope, the appearing of the glory of our great
God and Savior Jesus Christ, who gave himself for us to redeem us
from all lawlessness and to purify for himself a people for his own
possession who are zealous for good works. (Titus 2:11–14)*

THE CHRISTIAN LIFE starts with hope in Christ, continues
with hope in the promises of God, and looks forward to the day
when our hope becomes sight. The return of Christ is called "our
blessed hope" (Titus 2:13). No matter how bleak a season you
are in, a happy day is coming—the King of Kings will come again.

Many times the Bible gives our hearts specific targets of hope
regarding the return of Christ. Imagine your heart is a chest full of
biblical expectations for Jesus's second coming. What would be
some items in your chest?

Relief. In his second letter to the Thessalonian church, Paul
says, "God considers it just to repay with affliction those who
afflict you, and *to grant relief* to you who are afflicted as well as to
us, when the Lord Jesus is revealed from heaven with his mighty
angels" (2 Thess. 1:6–7). All hardships will end once and for all
when the Lord returns, and Christians will be vindicated by God.

Justice. Although earthly justice systems break down, King
Jesus will reign down full, complete, and final justice when he
returns to the earth (see 2 Thess. 1:6–10).

Healing. Cycles of sickness and wellness will finally stop,
because when Christ returns, we will be finally and forever healed.

Paul writes, "The trumpet will sound, and the dead will be raised imperishable" (1 Cor. 15:52).

Rewards. We are saved completely by grace, and even our best works happen as we are strengthened by his grace. But the Bible speaks a lot about the righteous receiving rewards when Jesus returns. Clearly, these rewards are meant to motivate us to live for him more and more (see 2 Cor. 5:6–10; 2 Tim. 4:6–8).

Worship. When Jesus appears, we will see our Savior as he is. We will honor him without sin distracting us from him (see Rev. 19:6–8).

Holiness. When Jesus returns, his children will become like him. Christians will never again disobey God's commands in word, deed, attitude, thought, or motivation (see 1 John 3:1–3).

No wonder the return of the Lord Jesus Christ is called the Christian's *blessed hope.*

Reflect: Have you spent enough time meditating on the second coming of Jesus Christ? How does hoping for his return affect the way you live now?

Act: Look up all the Scripture passages listed in today's devotional. Use each category of hope for Christ's future return to form prayers of thanksgiving and specific requests for your life.

DAY 30

Heaven on Earth

For I consider that the sufferings of this present time are not worth comparing with the glory that is to be revealed to us. For the creation waits with eager longing for the revealing of the sons of God. (Rom. 8:18–19)

PART OF GETTING older seems to include falling apart. As our bodies fall apart, we also watch the world fall apart. In Romans 8, Paul tells us that there is hope for ourselves and for the world.

When Paul compares present suffering to future glory, he declares that as bad as you may have it on earth, your experience of heaven will be so much better that you won't be able to measure the difference between the two realms. This is not to discount the massive suffering that some endure on earth—the Bible treats suffering with seriousness and sobriety (see 1 Peter 1:6; 2:20–21; 4:12–13). But heaven will be incomparably more spectacular than our suffering was horrible.

In Romans 8:20–23, Paul goes on to say that a Christian's death results in the Christian's spirit being separated from their body. When Jesus returns, your body will be raised and reconnected to your renewed spirit. When sin entered the world through Adam and Eve, the world was cursed to suffer decay and bondage. But this futile world has hope, just as we do. The world too will be renewed.

If you will have a resurrected physical body for all eternity, what are the implications for the world to come? You won't be in a semi-physical state on a cloud with a harp. You will need a solid-ground kind of heaven, and you will have it. It will be literally heaven on a renewed version of this very earth. It will be the whole world, resurrected.

Don't be concerned about heaven being reduced to earthiness. Remember that God made the world and called it good.

All the difficult things about living here are the result of sin and the curse, which will be eliminated. This world will be stunningly beautiful and easy to live in. There will be no more sin, death, or disease. There will be no more weeds. I doubt we will even be able to mess up our gardens!

God included suffering in his plan in part to help us to long for heaven. In Romans 8:22–24, Paul describes the cursed world and Christians living on it as though both are experiencing the pains of childbirth. As we endure the present effects of sin and suffering, we groan inwardly and outwardly. We long for something better. The pains almost compare to the contractions a mother endures as the baby gets closer. But even as the mother moans with agony, she has hope. Soon the baby will be resting in her arms. Soon the suffering will cease. Hope keeps her going. Hope keeps us going as well. We have the hope of eternity in heaven.

Reflect: Are you ever tempted to think heaven will be ethereal and boring? We will have real bodies and happy work to do for the Lord. We may get to do some of our favorite things from earth. But the best part of heaven will be the presence of God with his people (see Rev. 21:1–5).

Act: The Bible reveals truth about heaven for us to contemplate. God doesn't tell us all that we want to know, but he tells us enough to motivate us. Spend time thinking about what heaven will be like, then talk about it with a close friend. Share with your friend the riches of your meditation on heaven.

DAY 31

Ultimate Hope

And I heard a loud voice from the throne saying, "Behold, the dwelling place of God is with man. He will dwell with them, and they will be his people, and God himself will be with them as their God. He will wipe away every tear from their eyes, and death shall be no more, neither shall there be mourning, nor crying, nor pain anymore, for the former things have passed away." (Rev. 21:3–4)

IN HIS BOOK *The Weight of Glory,* C. S. Lewis used a fable to explain how the reality of heaven might be expressed. Imagine a woman and her son in a dungeon with only a shaft of daylight coming through a ceiling grate. This woman has a sketchpad and pencils, so she draws pictures to show her son the wonders of the outside world. Imagine seeing sketches of fields, rivers, mountains, and cities, with only your mother's words to help you to grasp what they are.

Similarly, we are unable to fully apprehend heaven's wonders, but God wants us to know something about it. In the Bible's final chapters, Revelation 21–22, the words used to describe heaven represent even better realities than their plain meanings. God speaks to our senses, which are limited to our dungeon-like reality.

In the time of the Bible, the sea was a largely unknown, scary place. In Revelation 21, the new earth is said not to have a sea (see v. 1), which may mean that in that wonderful place nothing will be unknown and scary.

The capital of the new heavens and the new earth will be new Jerusalem, a city compared to a bride adorned for her husband (see v. 2). God's dwelling place will be there, with his people (see v. 3). He will wipe all tears dry. There will be no more mourning, crying, pain, or death (see v. 4).

The city will look like a jewel (see v. 11): sparkling foundations and walls, golden streets, and pearl gates. God's glory will radiate fiery refractions and reflections all around. The city is said to have the dimensions of a 1,380-mile cube (see v. 16). The only other cube-shaped place in the Bible was the holy of holies, the place in the tabernacle and temple where God met Israel over the ark of the covenant. Perhaps the city will function as one huge holy of holies for all of us in Christ.

Nations will bring good things, but nothing detestable will ever enter (see vv. 24–27). A river flows from Jesus's throne down main street, nourishing the tree of life, which yields fruit every month and whose leaves bring healing to the nations (see Rev. 22:1–2).

The little boy in the dungeon tries to believe his mother's pictures. But one day, Lewis continues, the mother realizes her son has a major misconception. He thinks the outside world is filled with pencil marks. When she tells him there are no pencil marks in the real world, the boy's vision of the world goes blank.

The mother's pictures are accurate, but every place she has drawn is far more detailed, rich, and textured in reality than pencil lines could ever represent. In the same way, heaven will be so much better than you can imagine.

Reflect: Take heart because of the reality of heaven. What are you most looking forward to seeing in heaven?

Act: Read Revelation 21:1–4, 22–27; 22:1–5. Consider the details that the Holy Spirit has given us about what heaven will be like. Smile afresh as you read each new feature. Keep smiling as you thank God for telling you about what is to come.

Conclusion

YOU ARE LATE to meet your friend. As you pull out into traffic, you notice the gas needle hovering over the empty line. You try your best calculations to determine if the amount of gas remaining will keep the engine running until you reach your friend. You hope your car has enough gas, but your hopes are just wishes. You don't know whether you'll make it or not.

Earthly hope is limited to the best earthly resources we can marshal. Biblical hope is different—it provides certainty about positive changes in the future. As a Christian, you are confident because you have the massive resource of the living God and his true Word. Because this resource is *infinitely better*, this hope has *transforming power*.

You can face the darkest tribulation with a spotlight of joy. You may not know all that God is accomplishing through the trial, but you can smile with the certainty that he is at work, controlling the duration, intensity, and scope of the trial, down to the details. He will be with you each step of the way, as he promised, and he will amaze you with the glorious outcome of the trial. Hope provides power to do the next right biblical thing. It may be in heaven when you see all that he is accomplishing, but at that point, you will agree with Paul that the hardships can't even compare to the glory to come (see Rom. 8:18).

If your hope is restricted to limited resources, all your optimism will find an end. But because of Christ, God loves you without limits. He knows about your situation, and he cares for you. He has all the power he needs to bring you through it. On some nights the full moon shines brightly, lighting up the darkness. On other nights, the moon appears to be a sliver. When it is new, the moon is invisible. In spite of what you see when you look up, the moon is always present, circling the globe.

God, your heavenly Father, is always there too. Sometimes he seems so radiant and his promises leap off the pages of the Bible. At times like that, your hope shines brightly. Other times, God seems to be only a shining sliver or not visible at all. In those times, he is still present and is working his good will. He still cares. He knows your situation. He is your bright, shining hope. He will keep every one of his promises. Your future will be great, because God will make it great in his time.

Acknowledgments

IT HAS BEEN my joy to serve the Lord as pastor of Faith Bible Church in Sharpsburg, Georgia, since 1995. Aiming this flock toward hoping in God has been my joy in the pulpit and in personal ministry. I am grateful for a patient church family as we all seek to keep moving toward heaven together, bringing as many with us as we can.

I am also grateful to God for my wife, Lynn, and our sweet children, Charissa, Danielle, Chloe, and Josiah. We were delighted to welcome Joshua into our family as he married Charissa, and now they are bringing our first granddaughter into the world. They all have been a consistent encouragement to me in working on this book. It was a pleasure to have Charissa help me each step of the way to do the initial editing of this book. Her skills have been sharpened considerably while working as a reporter for *World* magazine.

Special thanks go to Deepak Reju and the team at P&R for allowing me to contribute to this fine series. Amanda Martin and Aaron Gottier provided excellent editorial help to make this a better book. Thanks, Amanda, for your patient kindness as you brought greater clarity to my work. Other books already released in this series have been a blessing to me and useful tools in our church's counseling ministry. May the Lord be pleased to continue to bless these works.

The Lord Jesus deserves all the credit for anything helpful in this book. He not only saved me and taught me what I know about hope from the Bible but is also the source of hope for all of us. To him be the glory!

Suggested Resources
for the Journey

Bridges, Jerry. *You Can Trust God*. Colorado Springs: NavPress, 1989. [In this brief book, Bridges uplifts the hearts of his readers by pointing them to God's character. This is a small sample of his larger work, *Trusting God*.]

Busenitz, Nathan. *Living a Life of Hope: Stay Focused on What Really Matters*. Uhrichsville, OH: Barbour, 2003. [To strengthen your hope in God, you need to understand more of what his Word teaches about his character and his promises. Busenitz does a great job of applying the Bible's teachings on hope.]

Jones, Mark. *Faith. Hope. Love. The Christ-Centered Way to Grow in Grace*. Wheaton, IL: Crossway, 2017. [Using brief questions and answers, Mark Jones helps his readers to understand and apply the Bible's teachings on the vital subjects in the book's title.]

Peace, Martha. *Precious Truths in Practice: Holding Fast to God When You Are Overwhelmed*. Bemidji, MN: Focus Publishing, 2019. [Navigating through a massive personal crisis, Martha Peace put her years of experience as a Bible teacher and biblical counselor into practice to honor the Lord. She tenderly shares those lessons with her readers.]

Spurgeon, C. H. *Beside Still Waters: Words of Comfort for the Soul*. Edited by Roy H. Clarke. Nashville: Thomas Nelson, 1999. [The prince of preachers had a wonderful way with words. Out of his own experiences of suffering, Spurgeon offers excellent comfort and encouragement from bite-sized portions of Scripture.]

Tada, Joni Eareckson. *Hope . . . the Best of Things*. Wheaton, IL: Crossway, 2008. [God has used Joni's fifty years of suffering after a diving accident to give her a powerful voice of hope for other suffering saints. Her many books and videos are treasures of God-centered comfort. This small booklet is a good place to start.]

**BIBLICAL
COUNSELING
COALITION**

The Biblical Counseling Coalition (BCC) is passionate about enhancing and advancing biblical counseling globally. We accomplish this through broadcasting, connecting, and collaborating.

Broadcasting promotes gospel-centered biblical counseling ministries and resources to bring hope and healing to hurting people around the world. We promote biblical counseling in a number of ways: through our *15:14* podcast, website (biblicalcounselingcoalition.org), partner ministry, conference attendance, and personal relationships.

Connecting biblical counselors and biblical counseling ministries is a central component of the BCC. The BCC was founded by leaders in the biblical counseling movement who saw the need for and the power behind building a strong global network of biblical counselors. We introduce individuals and ministries to one another to establish gospel-centered relationships.

Collaboration is the natural outgrowth of our connecting efforts. We truly believe that biblical counselors and ministries can accomplish more by working together. The BCC Confessional Statement, which is a clear and comprehensive definition of biblical counseling, was created through the cooperative effort of over thirty leading biblical counselors. The BCC has also published a three-part series of multi-contributor works that bring theological wisdom and practical expertise to pastors, church leaders, counseling practitioners, and students. Each year we are able to facilitate the production of numerous resources, including books, articles, videos, audio resources, and a host of other helps for biblical counselors. Working together allows us to provide robust resources and develop best practices in biblical counseling so that we can hone the ministry of soul care in the church.

To learn more about the BCC, visit biblicalcounselingcoalition.org.

Was this book helpful to you?
Consider writing a review online.
The author appreciates your feedback!

Or write to P&R at editorial@prpbooks.com
with your comments. We'd love to hear from you.